EASTON

OPPOSITE: This image shows Washington Street shops located across from the Court House Square in 1915. (Image courtesy of the Talbot County Free Library.)

Then & Now

EASTON

Mindie Burgoyne

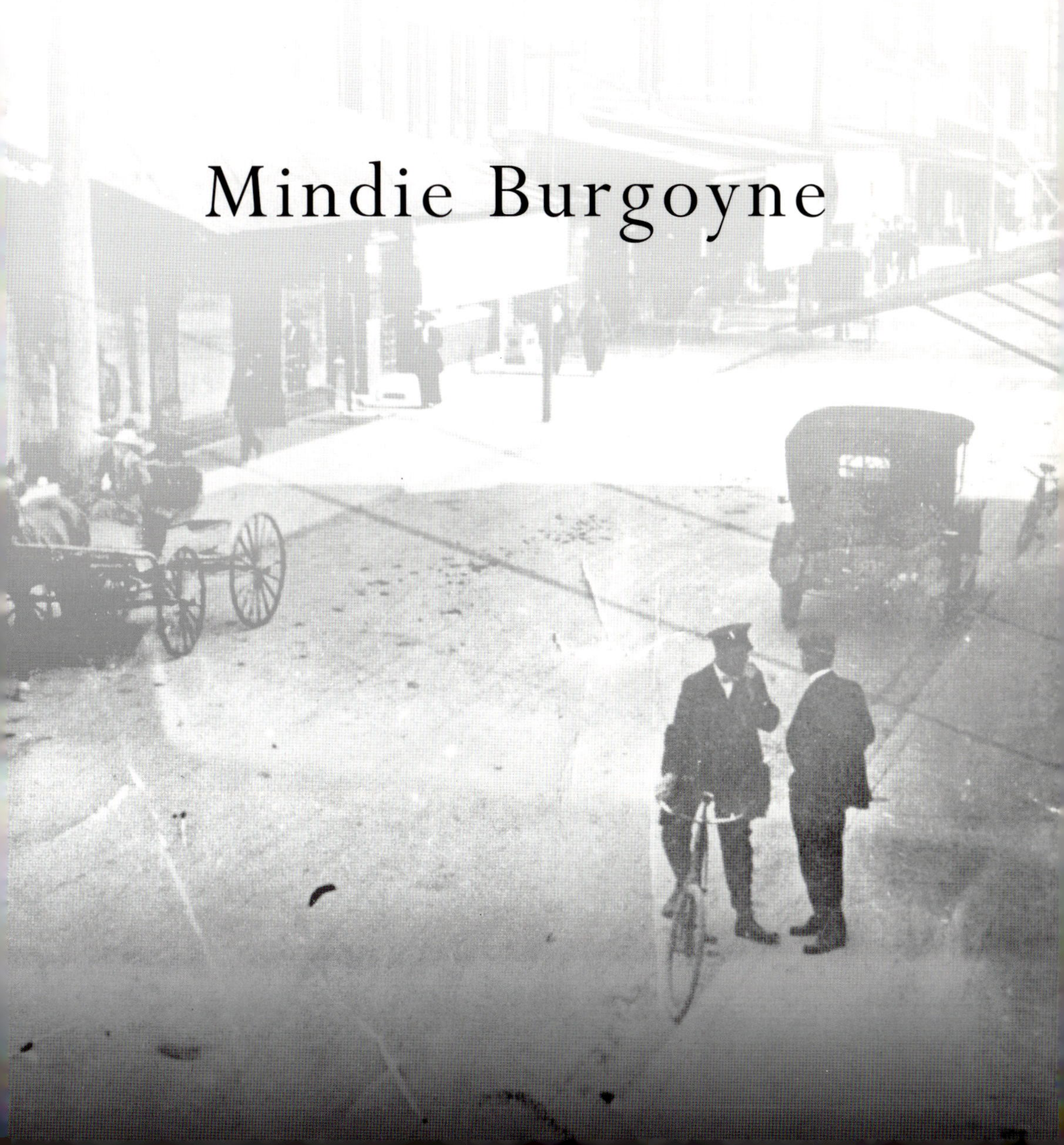

To Al Bond, Paige Bethke, and Debbi Dodson—my economic development partners and friends. You motivate me with your enthusiasm, creativity, and willingness to persevere through obstacles others see as insurmountable. Your faith in the Town of Easton inspires me. Your work and dedication is a great service to Eastonians today and those of the future.

Published by Arcadia Publishing
Charleston SC, Chicago IL, Portsmouth NH, San Francisco CA

Printed in the United States of America

For all general information contact Arcadia Publishing at:
Telephone 843-853-2070
Fax 843-853-0044
E-mail sales@arcadiapublishing.com
For customer service and orders:
Toll-Free 1-888-313-2665

Visit us on the Internet at www.arcadiapublishing.com

ON THE FRONT COVER: The intersection of Harrison and Dover Streets has been an anchor for entertainment and hospitality in Easton for over a century. Pictured here is the Avalon Theater prior to the 1930s and as it appears today. (Then image, courtesy of the Talbot County Free Library. Now image, courtesy of Mindie Burgoyne.)

ON THE BACK COVER: Pictured here is the Talbot County Court House as it appeared around 1900 after being remodeled for a second time in 1898. (Image courtesy of the Talbot County Free Library.)

CONTENTS

ACKNOWLEDGMENTS

The Town of Easton is alive with talent and enthusiasm for preserving heritage and remembering the past, which made writing this book so much easier than I had originally expected. I am indebted to the Talbot County Free Library and its Maryland Room staff, particularly the effervescent Monique Gordy, who selflessly offered her time, expertise, and sense of humor. Over half of the historic images in this book are from this remarkable facility. Additionally, I would like to thank Pete Lesher at the Chesapeake Bay Maritime Museum who offered the Laurence G. Claggett Collection for use in this book. It was an unexpected treat to work with Pete, who has brilliant mind and a humble spirit—two qualities rarely intertwined in the same person.

Polly Shannahan of Historic Easton, Inc.; Debbi Dodson and Nina Wahl of the Talbot County Tourism Office; Al Bond and Mayor Bob Willey from the Town of Easton; Priscilla Spence; Molly Bond; Dr. Laurence Claggett; Mike Henry; Marie Uren; Dave Ireland; George "Happy" Mayer; Scott Warner; John General; and Terry Deighan all assisted me in my quest for information about Easton, a town of which I knew little before starting this project.

Thank you to Larry Effingham, publisher of Chesapeake Publishing, who allowed me to photograph his employees during work hours. I thank my family and friends, whom I ignored and neglected for a month prior to this project's deadline.

As always, my deepest, sincerest gratitude goes to my husband, partner, and best friend, Dan Burgoyne, who spent countless hours following me around Easton, proofreading the manuscript, and patiently listening to me jabber on about Easton's historic points of interest long after I knew he was bored.

All images courtesy of Mindie Burgoyne unless otherwise noted.

REFERENCES

Beatty, Cynthia. *Historic Easton; Its History and Architecture.* Easton, MD: Historic Easton, Inc. 1979.

Buse, Elliott. *150 Years of Banking on the Eastern Shore.* Easton, MD: 1955.

Harrington, Norman. *Easton Album.* Easton, MD: The Historical Society of Talbot County, 1986.

Higgins, Martin. *History of the Reincarnation of Easton, Maryland.* Easton, MD: Star Democrat, 1926.

Ludlow, Hayman, John C. *Rails Along the Chesapeake.* 1979, Marvadel Publishers.

Patchett, S. Ellwood. *The History and Directory of Easton.* Easton, MD: Gazette Steam Book and Job Office, 1881.

Tilghman, Oswald. *History of Talbot County Maryland 1661-1861.* Easton, MD: 1915.

Weeks, Christopher. *Where Land and Water Intertwine.* Baltimore, MD: The Johns Hopkins University Press, 1984.

INTRODUCTION

Easton is currently the second largest town in the eight counties that comprise Maryland's Eastern Shore. Located in the center of eastern Maryland, Easton is the Shore's hub for culture and the arts, and it continues to thrive as a commercial center. There are 49 incorporated towns on the Eastern Shore, and most have quaint town centers that reveal residents' enthusiasm for historic preservation. But those towns pale in comparison to Easton's size and density of streets—both commercial and residential—that are lined with restored historic properties, projecting an authentic view of a thriving colonial town.

Easton, now a county seat, lies in the center of Talbot County. Recently, a fellow Maryland enthusiast quizzed me as to why county seats were located in the center of most counties. His explanation was that the center of the county was often one-day's horse ride, making it centrally convenient. While practical, being centrally located geographically was only part of the reason Easton became the county seat, and it was also the reason the town was so slow to grow at first.

On the Eastern Shore, colonial Marylanders didn't travel by horse; they traveled by boat, as waterways snake through the region, creating over 3,000 miles of shoreline. Seven of the eight county seats were assigned at active ports of call, such as Cambridge, Salisbury, and Snow Hill. Easton's circumstances of assignment were a bit different. Though the town rests on the northern branch of the Tred Avon River, that location wasn't a busy port at the time, and there were much larger, more active ports, including Oxford, Dover, and York. The Easton location was chosen as a compromise. It was central, on a waterway, and not a player in the heated controversy about which town should be the county seat.

Prior to 1680, general court on the Eastern Shore was held in private homes. In 1680, the first courthouse was built in Talbot County in the town of York, located near Skipton. In 1707, the county boundaries were redrawn and the York location became too far removed from the general population. The court relocated to the thriving town of Oxford, which was centrally located to most of Talbot County when traveling by boat. Oxford continued to act as the county seat with court held in private homes until 1710 when the Maryland General Assembly decided to purchase land in central Talbot County, known as "Pitte his Bridge," and authorized the building of a courthouse.

On this tract of land a brick courthouse measuring 20 by 30 feet was completed in 1712, and from there a small village slowly grew. An old Native American trail, which is now Washington Street, ran past the courthouse, but in the early 1700s, most people traveled by boat and lived and did business near waterways. Eventually, court offices, shops, and dwellings for officers of the court sprang up, and the village became known simply as "Talbot Court House."

As the village grew, the population outgrew the small courthouse. In 1777, an act of the general assembly designated the town of Dover on the Choptank River, just south of the Dover Bridge, to be the future Talbot County seat. That act was never carried out, and in 1785, a new act authorized the design and layout of an expanded town in Talbot Court House.

In 1788, the general assembly passed a law for holding general court for transactions and determining business of the Eastern Shore. In the same act, the town was officially named Easton. A year later, the general assembly authorized the building of a courthouse for which two-thirds of the funds for building costs were supplied. That courthouse is the same one seen today, though it has expanded as the population has grown over the last two centuries.

There is no official document or memoir that details how Easton got its name. But it is generally accepted that the legislature, by not only funding the majority of the new courthouse, but also by authorizing the foundation of a new town, meant for Easton to be a second capital, or the "eastern capital," of Maryland—possibly formerly referred to as East Town and later Easton.

Today court is still in session in the Talbot County Court House, which was completed in 1794, though courthouses exist in all eight Eastern Shore counties. Easton is still a bustling town, doing the business of government, finance, and, most recently, a robust hospitality and recreation business that attracts thousands of visitors each year. Easton has become a center for culture and an attractive destination for recreation with fine food, famous chefs, unique galleries, plush inns, and famous events, such as the Waterfowl Festival, the Plein Air Art Festival, the International Food and Wine Festival, and, most recently, the Chesapeake Film Festival.

Any day of the year, one can observe a new visitor walking the streets of Easton, marveling at the architecture, the streetscapes, and friendliness of the people who are having meals in outdoor cafes in good weather and scurrying into shops and restaurants when the weather is harsh. The town is a vast, historic wonder that has remained remarkably intact because of the dedication of generations of Eastonians who love their hometown and who work tirelessly to preserve its history and charm.

Oswald Tilghman articulated this sentiment in his writings, which chronicled Talbot County's history in 1915: "Many of the details here given may be, in the opinion of many, very trivial, and not worth the trouble of perpetuation in print; but to those possessed of the true antiquarian or archaeological spirit, nothing is unimportant that belongs to the past; to the student of history, whether it be the grand epics of nations, or the simple story of a county or neighborhood, nothing is valueless that is illustrative of the varying conditions of society; and by the lover of his natal soil, who with filial fondness cherishes every memento of the earlier days of the mother earth that bore him, nothing is disdained as insignificant that recalls the features of her prime."

THE COURT HOUSE SQUARE

When the Talbot Court House was built, it was the second largest structure in Maryland—the first being the state house in Annapolis. Its size, as well as the liberal funding for its erection by the state, lends credence to the story that this was to be the second capital of Maryland. This is the second courthouse built on this spot. (Image courtesy of the Talbot County Free Library.)

In 1898, the courthouse went through a renovation that extended it from five bays to seven. The town clock, which formerly existed in the pediment on the front of the building, was moved to the octagonal cupola. Additionally, a much-needed new jail (visible on right) was added to Court House Square in 1881. Today the seven bays are still the foundation of the Talbot County Court House complex, though the complex has been expanded. Frederick Douglas was the first African American orator to address a mixed race audience. He did so at this courthouse in 1836. (Then image, courtesy of the Chesapeake Bay Maritime Museum, Claggett Collection.)

COURT HOUSE AND JAIL, EASTON, MARYLAND.

1120   The Jail, Talbot County, Easton, Md.

The jail was constructed on the northeastern end of the courthouse complex. It also housed the sheriff and his family, who provided meals for prisoners. The jail has survived the complex's renovations and expansions. The image below shows the rear of the jail with a recent addition. Today it is part of the courthouse complex and houses the office of the Talbot County state's attorney. (Then image, courtesy of the Chesapeake Bay Maritime Museum, Claggett Collection.)

MUSIC HALL, PLAZA AND COURT HOUSE, EASTON, MD.

The Music Hall and Plaza was built in 1879 and was used as both a cultural center and a commercial, open market. It was part of Court House Square, bordered by Dover Street on the south side and Market Street, running between the hall and the courthouse. Today Market Street has been consumed by the courthouse expansion. The music hall was converted into the Talbot County Free Library and eventually became part of the courthouse building. (Then image, courtesy of the Chesapeake Bay Maritime Museum, Claggett Collection.)

The Talbot County Court House, pictured below in 1930, has its columned portico, which vanished in the renovations of the 1950s. At the time of this photograph, the courthouse was becoming inadequate for the demands of use. World War II and disagreements on how to handle an expansion delayed renovations until 1958 when two wings connected by hyphens on the north and south sides were added, preserving the "park-like" setting of the original complex. (Then image, courtesy of the Talbot County Free Library.)

These aerial views of Court House Square show the transformation when the music hall and the jail were incorporated into north and south wings, connected by hyphens. There was much angst among residents in determining how to expand the courthouse to meet the demands of a growing community in a way that did not destroy the beauty of the square, as well as how to preserve the jail and incorporate it into the expanding complex. (Then and Now images, courtesy of the Talbot County Free Library.)

In 1940, the music hall went through a transformation that forfeited the memorable, neo-Gothic roofline. Once completed, the transformed music hall housed the Talbot County Free Library, as well as other county offices. Today what was once the music hall has been meshed into the south-wing addition and serves as part of the courthouse complex. (Then image, courtesy of the Talbot County Free Library.)

This 1940s image shows the transformed music hall serving as the Talbot County Free Library. In 1976, a new library building was erected one block south. The current Talbot County Free Library houses more than 100,000 books and has three branches: Easton, St. Michaels, and Tilghman Island. Additionally, the library has a van that transports those who cannot get to the branches by other means. (Then image, courtesy of the Talbot County Free Library.)

CHAPTER 2

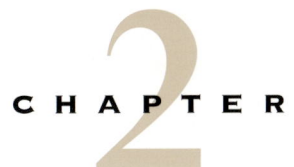

PUBLIC SERVICES

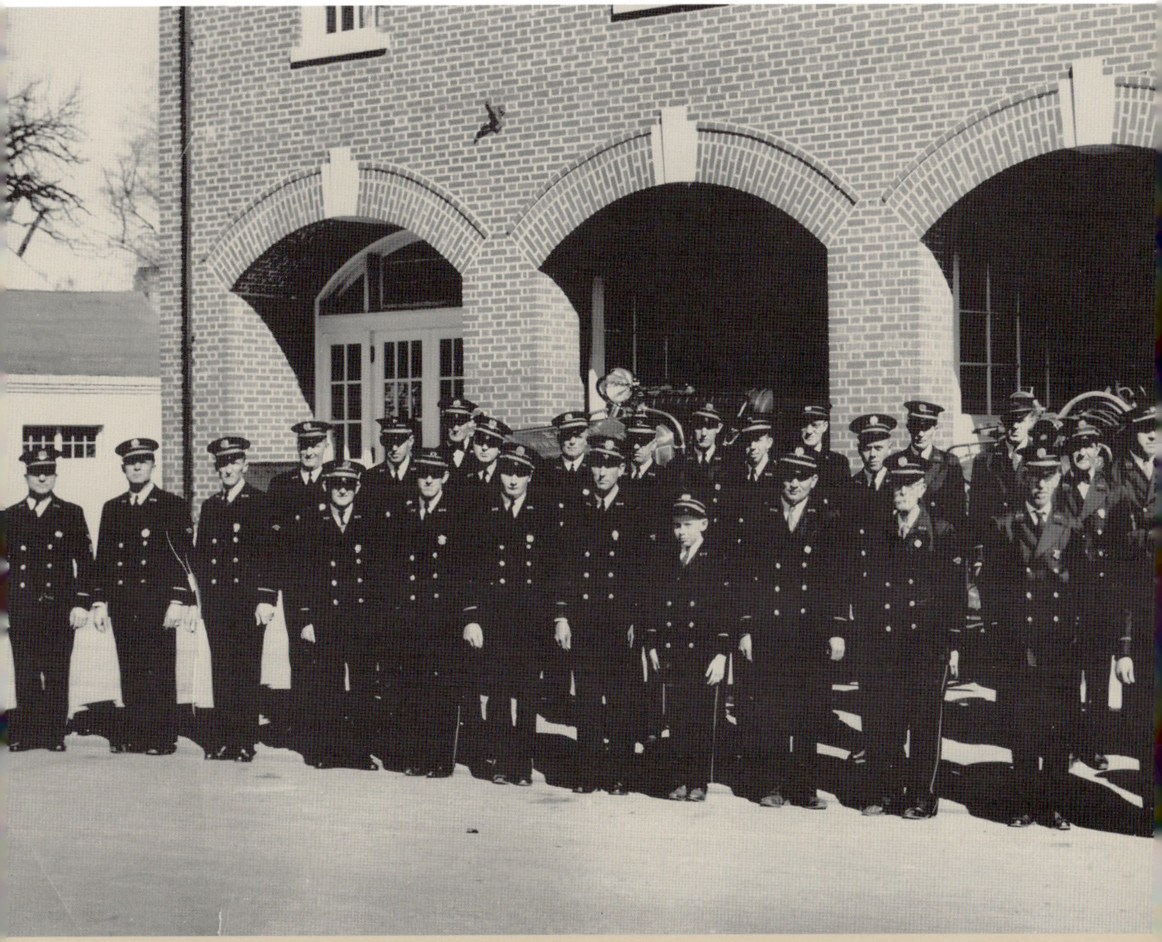

Easton firemen in 1933 stand for a photograph in front of their new engine house. The Easton Volunteer Fire Company was founded in 1808 and is said to be the oldest, continually operational fire company on the Eastern Shore. (Image courtesy of the Talbot County Free Library, Bodenstein Collection.)

The old firehouse on Harrison Street, pictured right in 1923, housed the Easton Volunteer Fire Company until a larger engine house was built directly across the street 10 years later. The old firehouse was converted into offices for the Easton town commissioners. Today it serves as the Talbot County Welcome Center, which houses the county's office of tourism. (Then image, courtesy of the Talbot County Free Library.)

The Easton Volunteer Fire Company is the oldest civic organization on the Eastern Shore. The new engine house, pictured above in the 1930s, eventually gave way to a new headquarters and engine house on Aurora Park Drive and Creamery Lane. The engine house was converted to offices and now serves as the Easton Town Hall. (Then image, courtesy of the Talbot County Free Library.)

This nickel-plated Silsby steam pumper was used by the Easton fire company from April 1914 through November 1920. Today the Easton Volunteer Fire Department operates from two stations with four engines, a tower ladder, a heavy rescue, a tanker, and numerous support vehicles. The department also has a dive team, emergency medical staff, and a fire-prevention education program with a 100 percent volunteer staff. (Then image, courtesy of the Chesapeake Bay Maritime Museum, Claggett Collection.)

The Easton Armory, which housed the headquarters for the Maryland National Guard, was built in 1927. It served the guard through World War II. The cannon, reputedly used in the War of 1812 to defend Easton from the British, has been relocated, and a stunning bronze waterfowl statue now stands at the entrance. The armory is home to the Waterfowl Festival, which attracts thousands of visitors to Easton each autumn. (Then image, courtesy of the Chesapeake Bay Maritime Museum, Claggett Collection.)

The Easton Emergency Hospital was founded in 1907 and was housed in leased space on Washington Street that was formerly the Hotel Norris. The hospital was to serve patients not only in Easton, but also in Talbot, Queen Anne's, and Caroline Counties. In 1915, it expanded and moved to its present location several blocks south. Today the old hospital is an office building with retail shops on the ground floor, including a popular toy store. (Then image, courtesy of Linda Laramy.)

EMERGENCY HOSPITAL, EASTON, MD.

Emergency Hospital.   Easton, Md.

By 1913, the small Easton Emergency Hospital was overcrowded, having as many as 34 beds in only 15 rooms. In 1915, a new, 52-bed hospital was dedicated, and expansions continued over the years. Today the Easton hospital has around 200 beds and provides emergency and specialized services, as well as outpatient services, for the Mid-Shore region. The hospital is now Talbot County's largest employer, with more than 1,700 employees. (Then image, courtesy of the Talbot County Free Library.)

This building at the intersection of South and Harrison Streets is actually two schoolhouses fused together, and it has a murky, undiscovered history. It is known that the buildings served as a primary school until 1929 when a primary school was opened in the old Easton High School. In 1933, the building was sold and converted to a funeral home. Today it has been expanded and completely renovated, and it serves as the Academy Art Museum, providing exhibitions, performances, and educational programs. (Then image, courtesy of the Chesapeake Bay Maritime Museum, Claggett Collection.)

The Academy at Easton was a private school established by the Maryland General Assembly in 1799. This building on Hanson Street served as the first public high school in Talbot County, opening in 1866. It was replaced by another high school building built in 1894. Today the Talbot County Health Department occupies this site. (Then image, courtesy of the Talbot County Free Library.)

This Easton High School building, built in 1894, replaced the Academy at Easton building on Hanson Street. It continued to operate as a high school and later as an elementary school until it burned beyond repair. Today Easton's public high school, on Mecklenburg Road, has over 1,100 students and has proved to be aggressive in educational progress. For example, it instituted a program that provided students with laptop computers. (Then image, courtesy of the Talbot County Free Library.)

HIGH SCHOOL, EASTON, MD.

This Easton High School was erected in 1929, built on a site where Idlewild Avenue, Harrison Street, Washington Street, and Oxford Road all come together around a square that was previously the Talbot County Fairgrounds. In 1954, the school was made into an elementary school, and in 1980, it was demolished. The site now houses Idlewild Park, which includes ball fields, tennis courts, rolling lawns, shade trees, and a new, enclosed playground. (Then image, courtesy of the Chesapeake Bay Maritime Museum, Claggett Collection.)

African American children in Easton attended the Moton School on Port Street, named for renowned African American educator Robert Russa Moton. The rear of this school is shown in the photograph above with children playing. The school was built in 1937 and was the first high school in Talbot County for African American students. It still stands today on Port Street but has been converted into apartments. (Then image, courtesy of the Talbot County Free Library.)

The Home of the Friendless, also known as the Children's Home of the Eastern Shore, is shown below as it appeared in 1890 with some of its orphaned residents posing on the lawn. This home housed orphaned children from all over the shore for more than 100 years. Once public social service organizations assumed the role of handling orphans, the home closed. It has since been enlarged and exists today as apartments in the same location. (Then image, courtesy of the Chesapeake Bay Maritime Museum, Claggett Collection.)

Across the street from the children's home stood the Home for Aged Ladies at 108 North Higgins Street. When elderly ladies were left to care for themselves, this home was a place of refuge where the women could live and be company for one another, and do both on sparse incomes. Today the house looks much the same. It has been renamed the Dixon House and is an assisted-living facility for both men and women. (Then image, courtesy of the Chesapeake Bay Maritime Museum, Claggett Collection.)

Home for Aged Ladies, Easton, Md.

EASTON'S ECONOMY

This sign in an open field is an early indicator of Easton's efforts to attract business and industry, and would not apply today. Easton, still a center for jobs in the region, has five industrial parks, a technology center, an airport, and a small port. It is still an industrial, financial, and retail center for the Upper Shore. (Then image, courtesy of the Talbot County Free Library)

Since its initial growth as a town, Easton's anchor industries have been banking and finance. It is no wonder that the Easton National Bank was given such a place of prominence at the corner of Goldsborough and Washington Streets across from the courthouse. The Beaux-Arts style gave the building even more emphasis in the town. At one time, the Easton Post Office operated out of this building. Today Bank of America occupies the building. (Then image, courtesy of the Talbot County Free Library.)

This 1908 postcard view of the Talbot Bank on Dover Street was released shortly after the bank opened in this location. The building has changed little, save for an eastern expansion and the trademark rotating clock near the front entrance. Talbot Bank was chartered in 1885 and has operated continuously as an independent bank since its beginning. (Then image, courtesy of the Talbot County Free Library.)

The Talbot Bank, Easton, Maryland.

Easton became a financial hub of the Eastern Shore. Money was concentrated by virtue of the wealthy people that moved to the region. Shown below is the Liberty Bank, which opened on Dover and Aurora Streets in 1920. It was later expanded and given a brick makeover, becoming Union Trust Bank. Today the building operates as a community church. (Then image, courtesy of the Talbot County Free Library.)

This 1870 photograph above shows merchandise being delivered to Thompson and Kersey, a business located on Washington Street near Dover Street. The current image does not depict the same location, but both images show the brick row houses characteristic of Washington Street, which were originally built to allow commercial use on the ground floor and living quarters above. (Then image, courtesy of the Talbot County Free Library.)

The view in the historical image is taken from the second floor of the old music hall, which stood next to the courthouse (see page 14). It shows the old Market Square, nestled between Market Street on the left and Dover Street on the right. The buildings in the distance are on the corner of Washington and Dover Streets. The recent image, taken from the same perspective, shows how the courthouse expansion consumed the Market Square. (Then image, courtesy of the Talbot County Free Library.)

These images depict South Washington Street one block south of the courthouse. The 1910 image shows the emergency hospital on the left (with awnings). The steeple of Calvary Methodist Church is seen in the distance. Today the church has been razed, the hospital has been renovated for commercial and retail use, and the buildings that once stood on the east side of the block are gone, having been replaced by a community park. (Then image, courtesy of the Talbot County Free Library.)

This block of Washington Street lies directly across from the Court House Square and was the hub of commerce for the town in 1905. The brick row houses and facades look much the same because of an aggressive effort on the part of Eastonians to preserve the historic districts of the town. Today this block houses upscale shops, restaurants, and financial offices. (Then image, courtesy of the Talbot County Free Library.)

WASHINGTON STREET
OPPOSITE COURT HOUSE
SQUARE · 1905

Once the automobile became available to the general public, they could be seen parked all around the center of town in Easton. Ford Model T and other cars are seen in this 1925 image. The current image shows Washington Street from the southern perspective. The street is about the same width as it was 1925 with parking on both sides. Traffic can be heavy during the week. (Then image, courtesy of the Talbot County Free Library.)

William Shannahan stands in front of an Avery tractor for sale at Shannahan and Wrightson Hardware on Washington Street. The hardware store still stands today directly across from the courthouse front door. It is a reminder of the once-thriving business that provided hardware, wagons, farm machinery, trucks, cars, and all kinds of equipment. (Then image, courtesy of the Chesapeake Bay Maritime Museum, Claggett Collection.)

Cars were sold on the second floor of the Shannahan and Wrightson Hardware Company. Shown below is a showroom where Buicks were sold. Today the Bob Smith Automotive Group, also known as "the GM Giant," serves automotive needs for Eastonians and residents in five counties. They are the largest volume dealer in Talbot County and one of the largest in the state. (Then image, courtesy of the Chesapeake Bay Maritime Museum, Claggett Collection.)

Goldsborough Street has changed little since 1930, but the type of businesses located in the block are different. This block formerly included stores that sold hardware, drugs, furniture, men's clothing, and cars. An upscale coffee shop, fine restaurants, a pet-product store, and an Irish-product store are some of the shops that currently occupy the block. (Then image, courtesy of the Chesapeake Bay Maritime Museum, Claggett Collection.)

EASTON'S ECONOMY

William Carpenter's Fish Market was one block behind the Court House Square at 4 South West Street. The image taken in 1905 shows Carpenter displaying his catch with an oyster shack visible to the right. The small brick building stands today in the same place with the windows bricked in and the oyster shack gone. It is not in use. (Then image, courtesy of the Chesapeake Bay Maritime Museum, Claggett Collection.)

The Harrison Street Market pictured above in this postcard from 1905 not only still stands on Harrison Street, but also has been there since 1791. The building is the oldest in Easton for which there is a public record. The first Freemasons in Maryland met in the loft of this building. Today the building is an upscale decorating shop and studio. A plaque on the front of the building recognizes the building as the birthplace of Freemasonry in Maryland. (Then image, courtesy of the Chesapeake Bay Maritime Museum, Claggett Collection.)

EASTON'S ECONOMY

These two views of Dover Street looking east from Washington Street show a typical sign of Easton's progress—the addition of parking lots. With the increasing amount of cars coming into Easton in the last 50 years, there has been a struggle to provide enough spaces for cars to park without losing the historic integrity of the town. The building in the historical image with the Coca-Cola sign on its side has been razed. A parking lot for the bank occupies its space now. (Then image, courtesy of the Talbot County Free Library.)

Dover Street, East from Washington Street. / Easton, Md.

This building on Dover Street next to the Bullitt House was built in the early 1800s as a private home. It was later converted into Clark's Motor Inn Garage, which sold cars and did car repairs. Later gasoline was also sold there, as well as tires. The building was razed, and the lot it rested on is now the municipal parking lot. (Then image, courtesy of the Talbot County Free Library.)

The standpipe was a water tower built in 1886 by a private water company. Its height and decorative cap have made it a familiar Easton landmark on Hanson Street. The tower stands 100 feet high and is made of wrought iron plates. Easton developed a piped water system around 1886, and the standpipe provided pressure, being able to hold 800,000 gallons of water. Though it is no longer operational, it remains a structure of historic importance in Easton. (Then image, courtesy of the Chesapeake Bay Maritime Museum, Claggett Collection.)

The main newspaper for the Mid-Shore region is the *Star Democrat*, which operated from this Dover Street location from 1912 to 1949. Thomas Perrin Smith opened the *Star*, then called the *Republican Star*, in 1799. The newspaper was first printed as the *Easton Star Democrat* in 1896 after two papers merged under the co-owner and editor of the *Star*, J. Frank Turner. (Then image, courtesy of the Talbot County Free Library.)

In 1961, *Easton* was dropped from the title, and the *Star-Democrat* became a daily publication in 1974. In 1978, the newspaper moved to a large facility in the Airport Industrial Park. That facility now serves as headquarters for Chesapeake Publishing. Today the company employs more than 200 people and has four news bureaus across the Mid- Shore region. The recent image above shows some employees in front of the current headquarters. The image below shows the former location on Hanson Street north of the standpipe (shown on page 49). (Then image, courtesy of the Talbot County Free Library.)

Railroad service came to Easton in 1869, and with it, an economic boom began, propelling farmers, merchants, bankers, and families into prosperity. Evidence of this wealth is still visible in today's historic homes. Pictured below is the Delaware and Chesapeake Railroad, which ran trains daily from Clayton, Delaware, to Oxford. This Easton Station has been lovingly restored by Historic Easton, Inc., in its original location. (Then image, courtesy of the Chesapeake Bay Maritime Museum, Claggett Collection.)

The Baltimore, Chesapeake, and Atlantic Railway (BC&A) also came through Easton on its way from Claiborne, Delaware, to Ocean City. In the image above, Engine No. 1035 crosses the Tred Avon River on a wooden trestle. Today the trestle is gone but will be replaced as part of Easton's Rails to Trails initiative, which creates scenic trails where railroads formerly operated. (Then image, courtesy of the Talbot County Free Library, Bodenstein Collection.)

The BC&A Railroad Station in Easton was located just south of Maryland Avenue on Aurora Street and is now an industrial and commercial area. The old rail bed, now paved, stretches westward as an access road for residents. This rail line had a sense of romance about it. Town folk would come out to the lines to watch the trains carrying vacationers from the city through small towns, open country, over rivers, and finally to the Atlantic. (Then image, courtesy of the Chesapeake Bay Maritime Museum, Claggett Collection.)

The Easton Airport was established in 1942 as an auxiliary airfield. After World War II, it was deeded over to Talbot County and the Town of Easton jointly. It currently ranks as the second busiest airport in Maryland, with over 160,000 operations (takeoffs and landings) each year. Today the traffic at this airport is private aircraft, mostly composed of corporate jets and recreational airplanes. By October 2007, the Easton Airport, now owned by Talbot County, will have an operational FAA tower. (Then image, courtesy of the Talbot County Free Library.)

This postcard image below, postmarked 1912, shows work being done on a state road near Easton by two men on one truck with a manager watching. Today roads in Easton are maintained by the Town of Easton, the Talbot County Public Works, and the Maryland State Highway Administration, which has offices and a large facility in Easton. The recent image shows some of the Talbot County roads trucks in their garage near Easton Point. (Then image, courtesy of the Chesapeake Bay Maritime Museum, Claggett Collection.)

Working on the State Road, near Easton, Md.

The Easton Furniture Manufacturing Company was founded in 1899 and ran a thriving business, providing jobs for hundreds of Eastonians for more than 40 years. The company made high-end oak furniture. The factory was located on the rail line at Brooklets Avenue. Today the remains of the factory are gone, but the area is still industrial and commercial. The Rails to Trails line that runs along the old railroad bed, used by walkers and bikers, can be seen in the recent image. (Then image, courtesy of the Chesapeake Bay Maritime Museum, Claggett Collection.)

Pictured about 1900, the Norfolk Shirt Manufacturing Company stood on Aurora Street near Talbot Street. The building was later used as a furniture store, skating rink, and wholesale business. Eventually, the building was razed, and a brick office building and market now occupy the site. (Then image, courtesy of the Talbot County Free Library.)

Industrial properties, such as the furniture factory and shirt factory, naturally sprang up along the Maryland and Delaware rail lines, making for convenient export. The Abbott's Dairy Plant, located on Needwood Avenue just off Davis Street, distributed milk from local farmers. It also supplied milk for Abbott's ice cream. Today a beauty shop, nail salon, and architect's office occupy the building. (Then image, courtesy of the Chesapeake Bay Maritime Museum, Claggett Collection.)

ABBOTT'S DAIRY PLANT, EASTON, MD.

ABBOTTS DAIRIES

The old Coca-Cola Company building on Bay Street is a prime example of how Easton transforms old structures to accommodate modern uses, maintaining the town's historic integrity. Located blocks from the courthouse, this building has been updated, renovated, and improved. It now houses offices for the law firm Miles and Stockbridge, and for other professionals as well. (Then image, courtesy of the Talbot County Free Library.)

These aerial views—nearly a century apart—depict industrial spaces in Easton. Though they are not the same site, the transformation from wood-framed buildings on the rail lines in the historical image of the Furniture Manufacturing Company, to the brick and block buildings on the main roads in the recent image of Airport Industrial Park is repeated throughout the town's industrial land. Today Easton has five industrial business parks housing companies that provide jobs in numerous industry sectors. (Then image, courtesy of the Talbot County Free Library.)

Easton Point is located at the end of Port Street on the Tred Avon River. It is a relatively small port for such a large town, but Easton is one of the few towns on the Eastern Shore that did not grow as a result of being a major port. Easton Point is well remembered for the steamboat wharf shown in the earlier image. Today Easton Point has a marina and several industrial companies. (Then image, courtesy of the Chesapeake Bay Maritime Museum, Claggett Collection.)

Prior to the steamboat era, Easton Point was dotted with private homes and warehouses for lumber and produce. Today most of the land is used for industrial purposes, but many boats are docked in slips, as well as anchored in the harbor (as seen in the recent image). Several developers have expressed interest in redeveloping Easton Point to serve more recreational uses. (Then image, courtesy of the Chesapeake Bay Maritime Museum, Claggett Collection.)

The Talbot County Chamber of Commerce was established in 1965 with fewer than 50 members. Today its membership has swelled to 860. It has had several locations, including the small building seen in the historical image below, which was on Route 50. The present location, which offers video conferencing, a resource room, and a conference room, is located in town in Easton Plaza on Marlborough Avenue. (Then image, courtesy of the Talbot County Free Library.)

FAITH, HOME, AND HOSPITALITY

In 1682, the Religious Society of Friends purchased three acres of land and erected the second Quaker Meeting House in Maryland—the Third Haven Meeting House in Easton. The wood-frame building still exists today and is the oldest dated building in the state of Maryland. It is one of several buildings on the site. This image shows the last of the oak trees from the original oak grove. (Then image, courtesy of the Talbot County Free Library.)

Built in 1856, Ebenezer Methodist Church regally stood on South Washington Street one block from the courthouse. In the 1950s, the Methodist churches in Easton merged. The building was sold and the steeple removed. It was converted to a furniture store for a time and eventually was acquired by the Historical Society of Talbot County. The second floor has been beautifully restored as an auditorium by the historical society. (Then image, courtesy of the Talbot County Free Library.)

FAITH, HOME, AND HOSPITALITY

The Asbury African Methodist Episcopal Church brick building on Higgins Street was erected in 1876, though the congregation formed in 1836. It was the first Methodist Episcopal Church in Maryland to be named for Francis Asbury. The church building has not changed much over the years, but the surrounding houses have seen many improvements. (Then image, courtesy of the Talbot County Free Library.)

Redemptorist priests from Annapolis traveled to Easton by boat, which led to the establishment of the Catholic parish in Easton—SS Peter and Paul. The original church building on Goldsborough and Aurora Streets was built in 1868 and remained in use until 2005 when a new church building was built to accommodate the large parish, which now has more than 2,000 families. The old building is now occupied by St. Andrew's Anglican Church. (Then image, courtesy of the Talbot County Free Library.)

FAITH, HOME, AND HOSPITALITY

The Calvary Methodist Church steeple was visible down Washington Street well south of the Talbot Court House and a familiar presence in the Easton skyline. It was built in 1830 but sold after the Methodist consolidation in the late 1950s and eventually demolished. Today the Safeway and its parking lot occupy the site. (Then image, courtesy of the Talbot County Free Library.)

The Easton Episcopal Diocese was carved out as a separate entity from the Maryland Diocese in 1868. Easton became a cathedral city and the home of the bishop of the Easton Diocese. Trinity Cathedral was built on Goldsborough Street around 1876 from granite brought into Easton by boat. The steeple was a gift from Julia Hopkins Pickering and her husband. It was not added until 1978. (Then image, courtesy of the Talbot County Free Library.)

FAITH, HOME, AND HOSPITALITY

Trinity Methodist Episcopal Church was an imposing structure at the corner of Goldsborough and Harrison Streets. It was completed in 1876 and rested on the northeast corner of the intersection, with the entrance on Goldsborough. Like Calvary Methodist Church, Trinity was sold after the Methodist consolidation of the 1950s. It was demolished and site has had a gas station, a savings and loan, a bank office, and now hosts the headquarters of a private fast food business. (Then image, courtesy of the Talbot County Free Library.)

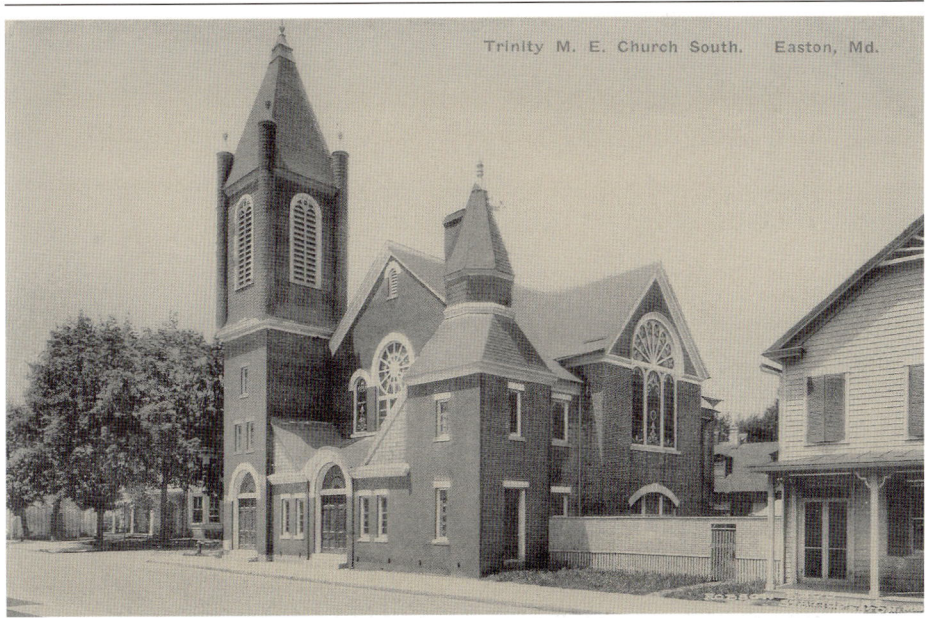

The Masonic Temple at 114 North Washington Street has occupied this spot since it was built in 1880, though the Masons were meeting in another location probably as early as 1749 (see page 46). It was built on the site where a now-defunct bakery and oyster house once stood. This was the home of Coates Lodge No. 102, named in honor of Dr. John Coates, founder of the first Grand Lodge of Masons in Maryland. (Then image, courtesy of the Talbot County Free Library.)

FAITH, HOME, AND HOSPITALITY

Two blocks south of the Masonic Temple on Washington Street is the Odd Fellows Hall at the corner of Washington and Dover Streets. This is the Miller Lodge No. 18 of the International Order of Odd Fellows, which met on this site starting in 1839, though this building was not constructed until 1879. Today the ground floor is prime retail space. Two earlier structures on this site were destroyed by fire. (Then image, courtesy of the Talbot County Free Library.)

The Langsdale House, named for a former owner, was one of four row houses next to the Masonic Temple on Washington Street. All four houses came under the threat of demolition in the 1970s, and a group of concerned citizens came together to save the homes because of their historic importance. That group became Historic Easton, Inc., which exists today, and the three middle houses were removed—one demolished, two relocated—to make room for a parking lot. (Then image, courtesy of the Talbot County Free Library.)

FAITH, HOME, AND HOSPITALITY

Similar public intervention saved this Federal-period house on South Washington Street, built *c.* 1804–1810. Recognizably one of the largest and most outstanding townhouses from the Federal period, this house, built by Quakers James and Rachel Cox Neall, was in danger of being razed in 1955. The group that united to save it became the Historical Society of Talbot County, which now owns the building and operates it as a museum and headquarters. (Then image, courtesy of the Talbot County Free Library.)

The Thomas Perrin Smith House at 119 North Washington Street was built in 1795. It is one of the most well-preserved Federal-style townhouses, displaying elaborate detail and craftsmanship. Perrin Smith was the founder of Easton's oldest newspaper, the *Republican Star*. He used this location as his office for many years. (Then image, courtesy of the Talbot County Free Library.)

FAITH, HOME, AND HOSPITALITY

The Trippe-Beale House, named for two families that have occupied the house, was built sometime shortly after 1851 when the design plans were drawn up by noted architect Richard Upjohn, who also designed the rectory of Christ Church. The unusual design with the jerkin roof pierced with wide jerkin dormers has made it a familiar Easton landmark on South Street. Today the house remains largely unchanged. (Then image, courtesy of the Talbot County Free Library.)

The Wrightson House, named for owner Charles T. Wrightson, sits on Dover Street near the intersection of Harrison Street. This Victorian-era mansion was built in 1874 and was sometimes referred to as "Captain's Watch" because of the balustraded widow's walk. The house has been a family home, apartments, and an office building. Today it is the Inn at 202 Dover, offering luxury accommodations to Easton visitors. (Then image, courtesy of the Talbot County Free Library.)

FAITH, HOME, AND HOSPITALITY

The Covington home on South Harrison Street is indicative of the wealth in Easton during the 19th and early 20th centuries. The *c.* 1920 image below is from a postcard that marketed the lovely homes of Easton. These large homes with wide, expansive lawns and deep lots straddle South Harrison Street today as they did 100 years ago. (Then image, courtesy of the Chesapeake Bay Maritime Museum, Claggett Collection.)

View on South Harrison Street, Extended, Easton, Md.

This Victorian-era house was designed for Benjamin F. Parlett by T. Buckler Chequier, a Baltimore architect. It was completed around 1890. Parlett was a wealthy Easton merchant, and wealth was evident on this part of Harrison Street both then and now based on the style of homes that occupy this section. Today the old Parlett home is the Fellows, Helfenbein, and Newman Funeral Home. (Then image, courtesy of the Chesapeake Bay Maritime Museum, Claggett Collection.)

ROBSON BROS.
STATIONERS
EASTON, MD.

RESIDENCE OF HON. B.F. PARLETT,
EASTON, MD.

FAITH, HOME, AND HOSPITALITY

BEAUTIFUL HOMES ON HARRISON STREET, EASTON, MD.

This house with its Greek Revival columns and portico is unique in Easton. It sits near the other large homes on South Harrison Street and once belonged to Judge William Mason Shehan. Today the house is still a remarkable landmark in this section of town, and though it is regal in stature, it still has the aura of a family home. (Then image, courtesy of the Chesapeake Bay Maritime Museum, Claggett Collection.)

"LONDONDERRY"

Londonderry was a land grant on the Tred Avon River that comprised much of where the town of Easton now rests. In 1867, a Gothic Revival manor house was built of stone brought by boat from Port Deposit. Part of this land was sold in recent years to develop a retirement community. Recently the Londonderry Retirement Community purchased the manor house and surrounding land to expand the community. The manor house will remain as part of the new development. (Then image, courtesy of the Talbot County Free Library, Bodenstein Collection.)

The Villa—now destroyed—was just outside of Easton at the end of Villa Road at the confluence of Goldborough Creek and the Miles River. It was built by rich New Yorkers and laced with legends about wild parties, gambling, and strange goings-on. Sadly, the Villa burned to the ground, and there is nothing left where it once stood. But the three-tiered fountain that graced its entrance has been moved courtesy of Joyce Delaurentis to Idlewild Park for all to enjoy. (Then image, courtesy of the Talbot County Free Library, Bodenstein Collection.)

Visitors needing lodging have been an integral part of Easton's history since the town grew around the courthouse. Today Easton's hospitality permeates the streetscape as it did years ago with hotels, inns, and places for refreshment. The Stewart building on Federal Street was formerly called "the brick hotel," as there was another clapboard hotel a block over. Today the Stewart building is a combination of retail and office space, and is about to undergo another renovation. (Then image, courtesy of the Talbot County Free Library.)

FAITH, HOME, AND HOSPITALITY

THE TALBOT TEA ROOM AND GUEST HOUSE
8 North Aurora Street
Phone Easton 450-W   Easton, Maryland

6524

The Talbot Tea Room and Guest House once stood on Aurora Street near the intersection at Dover Street. It was known for its plush interior and fine accommodations. It was razed to make room for yet another Easton parking lot and a drive-through for the bank. (Then image, courtesy of the Chesapeake Bay Maritime Museum, Claggett Collection.)

The Hotel Avon, later known as the Hotel Norris, was completed in 1891 and occupied the corner of Dover and Harrison Streets. The earlier image dates to 1905. The wagons in front ferried passengers from the steamboat landings and the railroad. In 1944, the hotel burned, and later the Tidewater Inn was built on the same site. The Tidewater Inn continues to be an upscale, popular place for accommodations, meetings, and dining out. (Then image, courtesy of the Chesapeake Bay Maritime Museum, Claggett Collection.)

FAITH, HOME, AND HOSPITALITY

The 1950s view of the Dover and Harrison Street intersection shows the Bullitt House and sign for the Tidewater Inn across the street. Today the Bullitt House still stands across from the Tidewater Inn, which has a new sign that matches its newly renovated interior and dining facility, named Restaurant Local. (Then image, courtesy of the Talbot County Free Library.)

The Hotel Queen Anne on Dover Street between Aurora and Hanson Streets opened in 1918. It served visitors during World War II. The hotel is now gone, but the Hotel Annex still stands and has been converted to apartments. (Then image, courtesy of the Chesapeake Bay Maritime Museum, Claggett Collection.)

QUEEN ANNE HOTEL, EASTON, MD.

FAITH, HOME, AND HOSPITALITY

The steamboat age swept through Easton in 1816, as it did most port towns on the Eastern Shore, carrying passengers from town to town or off to Baltimore. Easton Point had a steamboat wharf, and the *Talbot* was one of the grandest overnight steamers on the bay. Today the steamers are gone, and people travel the bay by personally owned boats, some of which are docked at Easton Point. (Then image, courtesy of the Talbot County Free Library, Bodenstein Collection.)

In 1920, Eastern Shore professional baseball heroes were photographed outside the Hotel Avon. They are, from left to right, Jimmy Foxx, Eddie Collins, and Frank Baker. Today Easton chefs known nationally and internationally pose in front of the Tidewater Inn. They are, from left to right, Gian-Carlo Tondin, chef of Scossa Restaurant; Michael Quattrucci, executive chef of Restaurant Local; and Daniel Tondin, chef of Mason's Restaurant. (Then image, courtesy of the Talbot County Free Library.)

FAITH, HOME, AND HOSPITALITY

CHAPTER

THE GHOSTS OF EASTON

Like any town, Easton has its ghosts. At least one is believed to reside in Dover Cemetery along the Choptank River. The cemetary has three graves, all of children. One grave, that of Samuel Harrison, who died in 1740 at age 13, is eerily marked with a headstone depicting a skull and batwings. Samuel's sister Rachel died at age five the year before and rests beside him.

All Saints Church was once a place of worship for Episcopalians just beyond Easton's northern limits. There are stories that the organ plays by itself, ghosts appear sitting in pews like worshipers on Sunday, and screams come from the bell tower. Today it is a private residence, and the owner states that his dog barks at the grave of three-year-old Willie J. Willis, who died in 1884, and that friends who mistakenly park on Nettie Beaven's grave immediately experience car trouble. (Then image, courtesy of the Chesapeake Bay Maritime Museum, Claggett Collection.)

ALL SAINTS CHURCH TALBOT CO MD.

The John S. McDaniel House on Aurora Street was once occupied by the colorful McDaniel, who fell on hard times and eventually took his own life. In recent years, the front door has been known to open and close by itself. The owner found a votive candle lit in one of the bedrooms while alone in the house. The next morning a fire broke out in that same room and caused major damage to the roof and tower. Today the home is a fully restored bed-and-breakfast. (Then image, courtesy of Mary Lou Karwacki.)

The Avalon Theater on Dover Street was built in the 1920s and has had a resident ghost for decades, according to some Eastonians. The ghost evidently likes to ride the elevator. Late at night workers still in the theater after events will report hearing the elevator door open, lights come on, and the elevator rising to the second or third floor on its own. They say it later makes its way down again with no one visibly on board. (Then image, courtesy of the Talbot County Free Library, Bodenstein Collection.)

Workers in the Talbot County Court House have reported strange happenings after working hours. The county emergency-management team once occupied the basement of the courthouse, and reports of toilets flushing, doors slamming, and footsteps in the hall were often delivered by workers on the nightshift. There was even a reported sighting of a prisoner stalking the halls and the grounds between the courthouse and the jail. (Then image, courtesy of the Talbot County Free Library.)

Across America, People are Discovering Something Wonderful. *Their Heritage.*

Arcadia Publishing is the leading local history publisher in the United States. With more than 3,000 titles in print and hundreds of new titles released every year, Arcadia has extensive specialized experience chronicling the history of communities and celebrating America's hidden stories, bringing to life the people, places, and events from the past. To discover the history of other communities across the nation, please visit:

www.arcadiapublishing.com

Customized search tools allow you to find regional history books about the town where you grew up, the cities where your friends and family live, the town where your parents met, or even that retirement spot you've been dreaming about.